I Love Sports

Baseball

by Allan Morey

Bullfrog Books

Bullfrog Books are published by Jump!
5357 Penn Avenue South
Minneapolis, MN 55419
www.jumplibrary.com

Library of Congress Cataloging-in-Publication Data

Morey, Allan.
Baseball / by Allan Morey.
     pages cm. — (I love sports)
Summary: "This photo-illustrated book for early readers introduces the basics of baseball and encourages kids to try it. Includes labeled diagram of baseball field and photo glossary." — Provided by publisher.
Includes index.
Audience: Age: 5.
Audience: Grade: K to Grade 3.
ISBN 978-1-62031-176-9 (hardcover)
ISBN 978-1-62496-263-9 (ebook)
1. Baseball for children—Juvenile literature.
I. Title.
GV880.4.H64 2015
796.357—dc23
                                          2014032107

Series Editor: Rebecca Glaser
Series Designer: Ellen Huber
Book Designer: Anna Peterson
Photo Researcher: Casie Cook

Photo Credits: All photos by Shutterstock except: Corbis, 16–17; Getty, 12; iStock, 5, 12–13, 16, 19, 20–21, 23br; SuperStock, 18, 23mr; Thinkstock, cover, 4, 8–9, 10, 14–15, 15, 23tl, 23tr.

Printed in the United States of America at Corporate Graphics in North Mankato, Minnesota.

Ideas for Parents and Teachers

Bullfrog Books let children practice reading informational text at the earliest reading levels. Repetition, familiar words, and photo labels support early readers.

Before Reading

- Discuss the cover photo. What does it tell them?
- Look at the picture glossary together. Read and discuss the words.

Read the Book

- "Walk" through the book and look at the photos. Let the child ask questions. Point out the photo labels.
- Read the book to the child, or have him or her read independently.

After Reading

- Prompt the child to think more. Ask: Have you played baseball before? Have you watched a game? What did each player do?

Table of Contents

Let's Play Baseball!

Grab a ball.

Put on your glove.

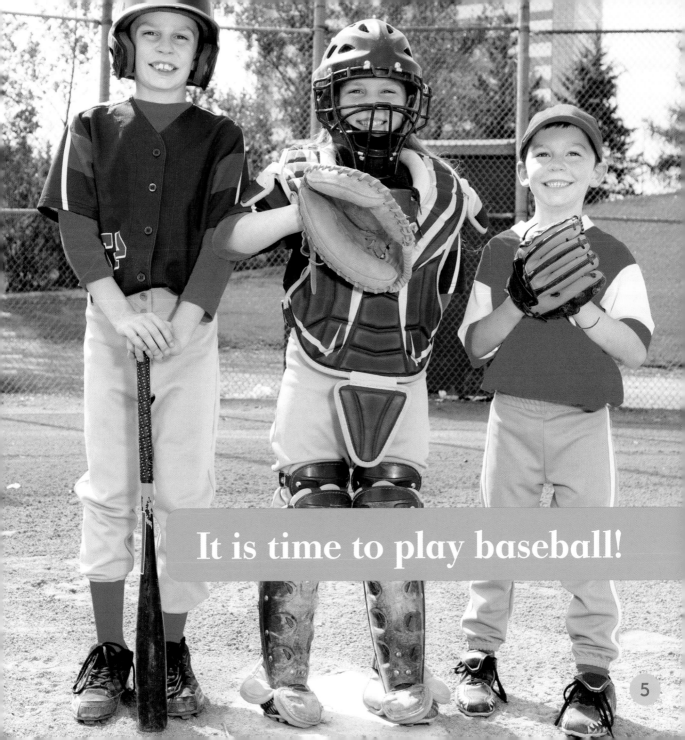

It is time to play baseball!

Tim plays on the Cubs.
His team is up to bat.

Lea plays on the Pirates.

She is the pitcher.

She throws the ball.

The batter swings.

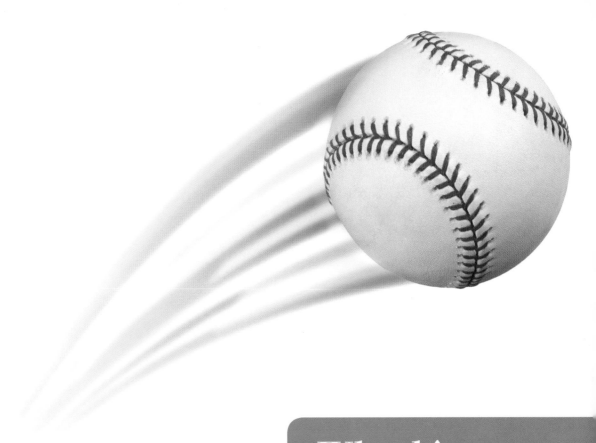

Whack!
The ball flies
into the air.

Kira plays in the outfield.

She catches the ball.

The batter is out!

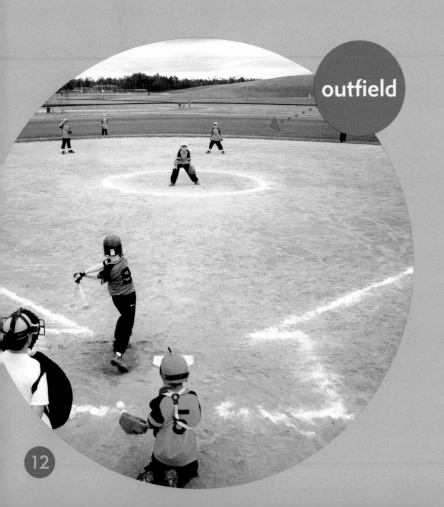

outfield

The teams switch sides after three outs.

Now the Pirates are up to bat.

Sam swings. Crack!

He runs to first base.

He races to second.

He speeds to third!

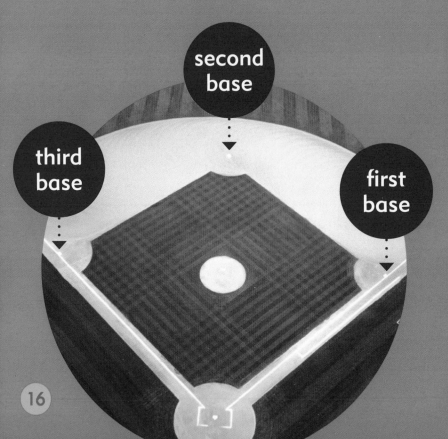

second base

third base

first base

The runner crosses home plate.

He scores a run.

home plate

The team with the most runs wins.

Do you want to play?
Take a swing.
Whack!

On the Baseball Field

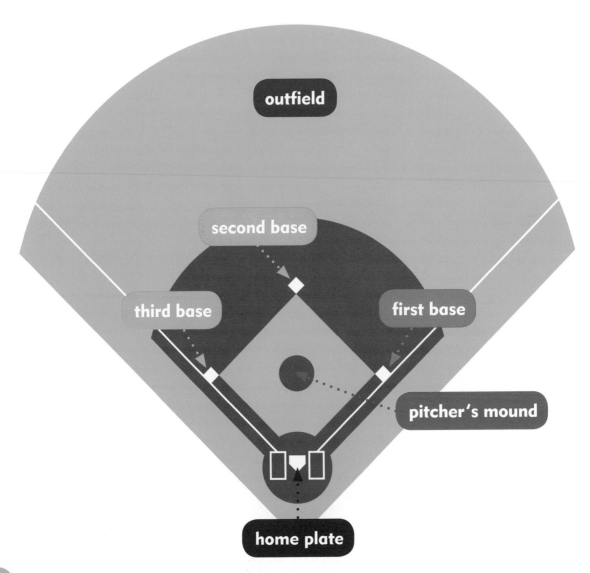

outfield

second base

third base

first base

pitcher's mound

home plate

Picture Glossary

batter
The player on a baseball team who tries to hit the ball with a bat.

pitcher
The player on a baseball team who throws the ball to the batter.

glove
A protective covering over the hand that a player uses to catch balls.

run
A point that is scored in a baseball game; the team with the most runs wins the game.

out
When a player's turn is over. If a player on the other team catches the ball, you are out.

team
A group of players who play together; there are nine players on a baseball team.

Index

To Learn More

Learning more is as easy as 1, 2, 3.

1) Go to www.factsurfer.com

2) Enter "baseball" into the search box.

3) Click the "Surf" button to see a list of websites.

With factsurfer.com, finding more information is just a click away.